We Can Get Along

A Child's Book of Choices

Lauren Murphy Payne • illustrated by Melissa Iwai

free spirit
PUBLISHING®

Library of Congress Cataloging-in-Publication Data
Payne, Lauren Murphy, 1956–
    We can get along : a child's book of choices / Lauren Murphy Payne, M.S.W. ; illustrated by Melissa Iwai. — [Second edition].
        pages cm
     Summary: "Using affirming language and full-color illustrations, this book teaches tolerance, kindness, and conflict resolution to young children. Includes activities and discussion questions for parents, teachers, and caregivers to use to further explore the topic with young children"— Provided by publisher.
    ISBN 978-1-63198-049-7 (hardback) — ISBN 978-1-63198-027-5 (softcover)
1. Social interaction—Juvenile literature. 2. Interpersonal relations—Juvenile literature. 3. Choice (Psychology)—Juvenile literature. I. Iwai, Melissa, illustrator. II. Title.
    HQ784.S56P39 2015
    302—dc23
                                                                                                        2015008010

Free Spirit Publishing does not have control over or assume responsibility for author or third-party websites and their content.

Reading Level Grade 2; Interest Level Ages 4–8;
Fountas & Pinnell Guided Reading Level L

Edited by Pamela Espeland and Alison Behnke
Cover and interior design by Colleen Rollins

10 9 8 7 6 5 4 3 2 1
Printed in China
R18860515

Free Spirit Publishing Inc.
217 Fifth Avenue North, Suite 200
Minneapolis, MN 55401-1299
(612) 338-2068
help4kids@freespirit.com
www.freespirit.com

To my family
with all my love and gratitude,
and for Scott, who always
has faith in me.

I know lots of people at school,
in my neighborhood,
and on the playground.

Sometimes we get along . . .

And sometimes we don't.

When we get along,
we talk together.

We laugh,
work,
and play together.

Sometimes we are quiet together.

When we get along, I feel happy and safe.

When we don't get along,
I feel angry and afraid.

I can remember my feelings
when I am with other people.

I can remember times
    when I felt happy or angry,
    safe or afraid.

My feelings can help me
make good choices.

I can think about my
words before I say them.

I can choose what to do
before I do it.

I am in charge of my words
and actions . . .

They belong to me.

I can talk and listen.

I can take turns and share.

I can help solve problems
and work things out.

I can do my part to get along.

friends

I know how I like to be treated.

I like to be talked to
and heard.

I like smiles and hugs
and friendly words.

I like to be treated with
kindness and respect.

Hi!

I can choose to treat others
the way I like to be treated.

GRRRR!

I know how I don't like to be treated.

I don't like to be teased,
called names,
or yelled at.

I don't like mean words.

I don't like to be pushed,

kicked, or bullied.

I don't like to be hit.

Hitting is never okay.

BREATHE

STOP

These things can hurt my body and my feelings.

Sometimes I feel afraid, or I get angry.

Sometimes I want to hurt someone back . . .

SLOW DOWN

CHOOSE

THINK

But I can choose not to do that.

When someone hurts me,
I can talk about my feelings.

I can walk away and
play alone for a while.

I can ask an adult for help.

These are good choices.

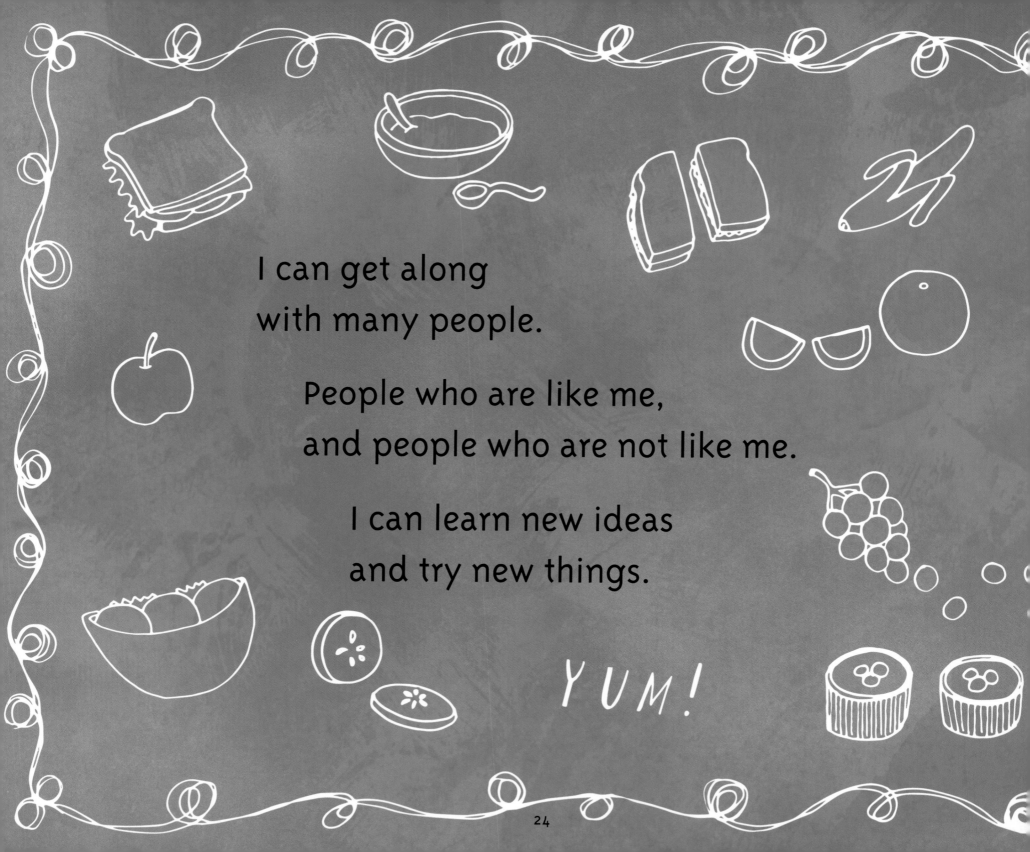

I can get along
with many people.

People who are like me,
and people who are not like me.

I can learn new ideas
and try new things.

YUM!

I can be a friend.

Friends are people
you can count on.

Friends are people
who talk to you

and listen when you talk.

Friends are fun to play with
and nice to be around.

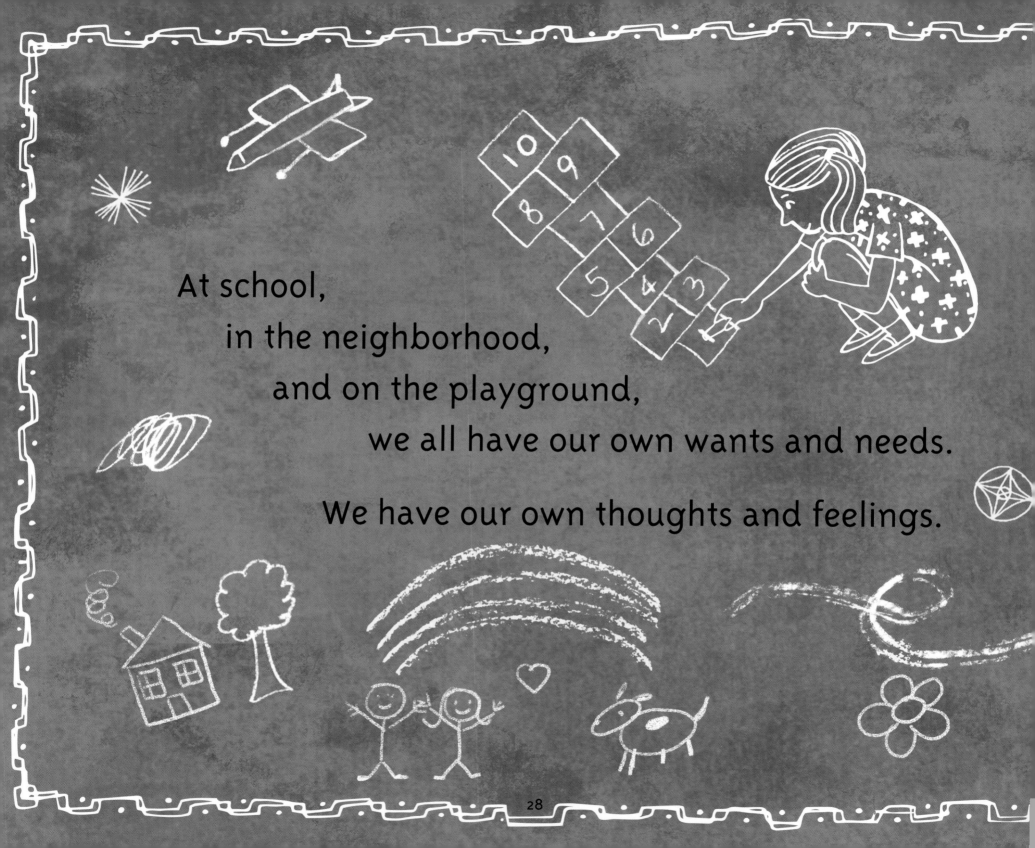

At school,
in the neighborhood,
and on the playground,
we all have our own wants and needs.

We have our own thoughts and feelings.

No two people are the same.

Even though we are different,
we can talk together.

We can laugh, work,
and play together.

Or we can just be quiet together . . .

We can get along.

A Note to Caring Adults

Conflict is a normal part of life for all of us—including young children. In any relationship, we will experience conflict at some point or another. As adults, we can help children learn how to deal with conflict positively and effectively. Children need to understand that they have the power to choose their words and actions. And when children recognize that their words and actions have consequences, they begin to learn responsibility.

We Can Get Along: A Child's Book of Choices can be read and enjoyed with young children in many settings, from preschool, school, and childcare to home, religious school, or a counseling group. Through reading, listening, creating, role playing, laughing, and loving, children learn that they are capable of getting along with others, making positive choices, and resolving conflicts peacefully. The book is based on the beliefs that:

❀ Children can learn to deal with conflict in healthy ways by learning to recognize their own reactions to conflict and by learning to identify their feelings.

❀ Children can learn that they are responsible for the things they say and do. They can learn to distinguish effective anger behaviors from those that escalate conflict.

❀ Children can learn to shift their focus in times of conflict from "How can *I* get what *I* want?" to "How can we *both* get what we need?"

❀ Children can learn that they can join together with others to find and create solutions that resolve conflict effectively.

❀ Children need to know that hitting is *never* okay.

❀ Children need to be empowered to remove themselves from hurtful or harmful situations.

❀ Children need to learn and understand the inherent value of all individuals, without regard to their differences or similarities.

❀ Children can learn how to respect the opinions of others and learn from them.

The activities and discussion starters that follow build on these core beliefs, and offer a variety of ways to teach the concepts and achieve the goals of this book. They are meant to be flexible, so feel free to expand or adapt them. Do whatever works best for the children in your group. The goal of using these ideas with children is not to control or define their behavior. There is no *right* way to learn how to get along with others, and there are no *right* answers to the questions. Instead, these questions and activities allow children to explore their own ideas and discover their own best ways of learning.

I encourage you to use your own instincts, creativity, and imagination when using this book. And last but not least: Remember to have fun! If children see you enjoying this book and these activities, they will, too. After all, what could be more fun and rewarding than learning how to get along with others?

—Lauren Murphy Payne, MSW, LCSW

Discussion Starters and Activities

Recognizing and Talking About Feelings

Ask children to think about times when they felt happy and safe. Talk about those experiences, asking questions like:

❁ Where were you?

❁ Who were you with?

❁ What were you doing?

❁ What felt safe to you?

Expand the discussion to consider broader ideas of these feelings. Ask questions such as:

❁ What are some things that help you feel happy and safe?

❁ Who are some people you trust?

❁ Who are some people you can talk to when you want to talk?

❁ Who helps you when you need help?

Continue this exploration with similar questions about other feelings. When is a time children felt angry or afraid? Excited or pleased? Worried or upset?

Coping with Hurt Feelings

Ask children to describe how they feel when someone calls them a bad name or says mean words to them. List their feelings on poster paper. Ask, "When someone says mean words to you, what can you do?" Help children brainstorm ideas and list

them on a second piece of paper. Have each suggestion begin with "I can . . ."

Asking for Help

Emphasize to children that asking for help when they need it is a good choice, and that there are grown-ups who can help them cope with situations and deal with their feelings. Invite children to think about adults they could ask for help, such as teachers, parents, grandparents, other family members, or counselors (at school or elsewhere).

Using I-Messages

Introduce I-messages to children. You might say something like the following:

Sometimes we don't feel happy and safe when we are with another person. We may feel sad or angry or upset. We need to tell the other person how we feel. And we need to do this without blaming the other person. When we say things like, "*You make me sad*," we are blaming the other person. That can lead to an argument.

There's a better way to tell someone how you feel and what you need or want from the person. You can use something called an I-message. Instead of saying *you*, start off by saying *I*. Here are some examples:

❀ "I feel sad when you don't want to play with me."

❀ "I feel angry when you can't share your toys."

❀ "I want you to stop making faces at me."

❀ "I need you to share the ball or I can't play."

After explaining the idea, present children with examples of situations where I-messages would be helpful. For example, "Hector is upset because he wants his older brother to play a game with him, but his brother says he doesn't feel like it. How can Hector use an I-message to tell his brother how he's feeling?"

Have children suggest different I-messages for each situation, or invite them to act out these scenarios using puppets, dolls, or action figures.

Agree to Disagree

Invite children to role-play situations in which they might agree to disagree. Children can act out scenes themselves or use dolls, puppets, or action figures. You can use the following scenarios or invent your own.

❀ Su Li loaned William one of her favorite drawings a long time ago, and now she wants it back. But William says he already gave it back. Su Li can't find it and William doesn't have it.

❀ Erik and Ahmed are building a tower out of blocks. Erik says he knows the best way to do it, but Ahmed thinks his own idea is better.

❀ Juanita and Stephan are best friends who both love baseball. Juanita likes the Yankees, but Stephan likes the Braves.

Drawing Together

Group children in pairs and give each pair a large sheet of paper, as well as crayons or colored pencils. Tell them that they are going to work together to draw and color a picture based on one of the ideas in the book. For example, "When someone hurts me, I can talk about my feelings" or, "Friends are people you can count on." If desired, give children the choice of a few ideas to choose from. Ask them to talk together and agree on the kind of picture they want to make. As they prepare to get started, ask questions like:

❁ What do you want to draw?

❁ What do you think your partner wants to draw? How can you find out?

❁ How can you make sure the picture is something you both want to draw?

Give children time to make their drawings. Remind them that friends work together, help each other, listen to each other, solve problems together, and find solutions when they don't agree. Afterward, invite children to talk about how they worked together. What did they like best about doing this activity with their partners?

Positive Choices

Offer children several hypothetical situations. For example, "You see Robert fall in a mud puddle," and three possible choices for a response or solution ("You help Robert up," "You let a teacher know that Robert fell," or "You and other children laugh at Robert"). Have children discuss which choices they think are best, and why. Help children empathize with the children in each scenario. Ask questions like, "How would you feel if you were Robert?" "What do you think you would want someone to do if you were in Robert's place?" "How do you think Robert would feel if someone laughed at him?"

Lists About Friendship and Feelings

You can use all of the following lists as starting points for conversations about feelings, conflict, and getting along with others. Read the lists aloud to children. You may also display images to represent list items and help young children understand them. You'll find suggestions for additional activities following each list.

12 Things Friends Do

❁ Play together.

❁ Stick up for each other.

❁ Listen to each other.

❁ Share feelings with each other.

❁ Talk together.

❁ Laugh together.

❁ Use kind words.

❁ Say "I'm sorry" when they say or do hurtful things.

❁ Help and encourage each other.

❁ Treat each other with respect.

❁ Share quiet times.

❁ Know that it's okay sometimes to disagree with each other.

Share the list with children and invite them to think and talk about it. Then help children put together their own list of things that friends do. Talk about why each item is important to them. Next, have children take turns doing short, wordless role plays based on ideas from the list. Ask other children to interpret what the role players are doing that friends do. Ask the role players questions about their actions. (For example, "How did it feel to do those things together?") Talk with children about times when they have done these things with friends.

12 Things Friends Don't Do

❋ Hit each other.

❋ Kick, scratch, pinch, or bite each other.

❋ Bully each other.

❋ Yell at each other.

❋ Break each other's things.

❋ Say mean things.

❋ Tease each other.

❋ Try to get their way all the time.

❋ Use bad language.

❋ Call each other bad names.

❋ Boss each other around.

❋ Exclude other friends.

Share the list with children and invite them to share examples of times when they have experienced any of the things on the list. Be clear and firm that they should not name any names or blame others. Ask children questions like, "How did you feel when that happened to you?" "What did you do when that happened?" Ask children if they have ever done any of these things. What happened? How did their friends react? Encourage children to think and talk about how they could use ideas from the book to help them deal with similar situations. Invite children to role-play these situations using dolls, puppets, or action figures.

10 Healthy Ways You Can Express Anger

❋ Tell someone you're angry.

❋ Hit a pillow or a bed with your fist, or pound on the floor with a rolled up newspaper or magazine.

❋ Jump up and down.

❋ Cry.

❋ Squeeze play dough or clay.

❋ Walk away.

❋ Sing an angry song or do an angry dance.

❋ Run.

❋ Ask for a hug.

❋ Go into a room where you feel safe to get some quiet time.

Talk about this list and invite children to add their own ideas. Then, if your space allows, have children find their own places where they can safely move around. Ask children to act out examples of ways to express anger from the list. Finish the activity by having children find a space to sit or even lie down quietly. Ask them to close their eyes and focus on their breathing. Have children work to slow down their breathing. Once they have quieted down, ask questions like, "What did that feel like to you?" "Do you think you would be able to do that if you were really mad?" "Do you think that could help you get your 'mad' out?"

As a group, brainstorm similar lists of ways to express and deal with sadness, fear, and other emotions.

10 Healthy Things You Can Do Instead of Hurting Someone

❁ Tell the person, "Please stop that. I don't like that!"

❁ Tell yourself, "It's okay to be angry. It's *not* okay to hurt someone else, even if that person hurt me first."

❁ Walk or run away.

❁ Take a deep breath and then blow it out slowly. Think about blowing angry feelings out of your body.

❁ Tell the person how you feel. Use an I-message.

❁ Find an adult. Tell the adult what happened and how you feel.

❁ Count backward from 10 to 1. Picture your anger getting smaller and smaller as the numbers do.

❁ Remember that hurting someone back *always* makes the conflict worse.

❁ Spend time somewhere safe and comfortable until you feel better.

❁ Remember that you are in charge of your own actions. You can decide what to do.

After talking about the list, help children think of times when others have hurt their feelings. Invite them to share as much as they're comfortable sharing. Ask children how they felt when that happened. Then help them think of times when they have hurt others, and invite them to think about how they would have felt if that had happened to them. Help children understand that no one likes to be hurt, and that hurting someone is never okay, even if that person hurt them first.

Give children drawing paper and crayons or colored pencils. Have them draw pictures that symbolize how they felt when they were hurt. They can draw representations of things such as volcanoes or tornadoes, or they can simply scribble or make patterns. Ask children to close their eyes and imagine their pictures in their minds. Out loud, count backward from 10 to 1. Tell children to make the pictures in their minds get smaller and smaller as you get closer to 1. After you reach 1, allow children to open their eyes, crumple up their anger drawings, and throw them away. Talk with children about how this felt, and help them understand that they can use this idea themselves when they need to.

What to Do If You Suspect That a Child Is Being Abused

If you are working in a school, follow the established protocols of your school and district immediately. You can also contact your local social service department or child welfare department, or obtain information about what to do and how to report child abuse from your local police department or district attorney's office. *Never* attempt to interview a child yourself. Instead, leave that to professionals who have been specially trained to deal with this sensitive issue.

About the Author

Lauren Murphy Payne, MSW, LCSW, is a psychotherapist in private practice with 30 years of experience. She specializes in the treatment of adult survivors of childhood sexual abuse, relationship issues, anxiety, depression, and eating disorders. Lauren has been a speaker at local, regional, and national conferences. She is the author and presenter of two video series: *Making Anger Work for You* and *Anger as a Fear Driven Emotion*. She is the mother of two adult children and lives in Wisconsin with her husband.

About the Illustrator

Melissa Iwai received her BFA in illustration from Art Center College of Design in Pasadena, California. She lives in Brooklyn, New York, and has illustrated many picture books, which can be seen at www.melissaiwai.com.

Other Great Books from Free Spirit

Just Because I Am
A Child's Book of Affirmation
by Lauren Murphy Payne, illustrated by Melissa Iwai
36 pp., color illust., HC & PB, 11¼" x 9¼". Ages 4–8.

F Is for Feelings
by Goldie Millar and Lisa Berger, illustrated by Hazel Mitchell
40 pp., color illust., HC & PB, 11¼" x 9¼". Ages 3–8.

Talk and Work It Out
by Cheri J. Meiners, M.Ed., illustrated by Meredith Johnson
40 pp., color illust., PB, 9" x 9". Ages 4–8.

I'm Like You, You're Like Me
A Book About Understanding and Appreciating Each Other
by Cindy Gainer, illustrated by Miki Sakamoto
48 pp., color illust., HC & PB, 11¼" x 9¼". Ages 3–8.

Interested in purchasing multiple quantities and receiving volume discounts?
Contact edsales@freespirit.com or call 1.800.735.7323 and ask for Education Sales.

Many Free Spirit authors are available for speaking engagements, workshops, and keynotes.
Contact speakers@freespirit.com or call 1.800.735.7323.

For pricing information, to place an order, or to request a free catalog, contact:

Free Spirit Publishing Inc. • 217 Fifth Avenue North • Suite 200 • Minneapolis, MN 55401-1299
toll-free 800.735.7323 • local 612.338.2068 • fax 612.337.5050
help4kids@freespirit.com • www.freespirit.com